Starting
Ukulele
the next step

Starting Ukulele
the next step

The number one method for
the advancing ukulele player

by Steven Sproat

WISE PUBLICATIONS
part of The Music Sales Group
London / New York / Paris / Sydney / Copenhagen / Berlin / Madrid / Hong Kong / Tokyo

Published by

Wise Publications

14-15 Berners St, London, W1T 3LJ, UK

Exclusive Distributors:

Music Sales Limited

Distribution Centre, Newmarket Road, Bury St Edmunds,

Suffolk, IP33 3YB, UK.

Music Sales Corporation

257 Park Avenue South, New York, NY10010, USA.

Music Sales Pty Limited

20 Resolution Drive, Caringbah, NSW 2229, Australia.

Order No. AM1003871

ISBN 978-1-78038-252-4

This book © Copyright 2012 Wise Publications,

a division of Music Sales Limited.

Original design: Kathy Gammon

Project editor: Lizzie Moore

Photography: Matthew Ward

Models: Holly Petrie and Tom Billington

With thanks to Chappell of Bond Street, London.

Ukulele: Steven Sproat

CD mastered by Jonas Persson

Tracks 9-10 produced by Gavin Underhill

Tracks 14-15 produced by David Pickering Pick

Tracks 18-22 programmed by Jonas Persson and Rick Cardinali

Tracks 24-25 arranged by Paul Buck. Produced by David Pickering Pick

Printed in the EU.

www.musicsales.com

Contents

No Longer A Beginner!

Welcome to *Starting Ukulele: The Next Step.*

Since my last book a few years ago I've taken many more ukulele classes and workshops both in the UK and overseas and have included in this new book some of the exercises, tips and techniques that people have found helpful.

I would like, in particular, to share a few techniques which once mastered bring a lot of pleasure and satisfaction to the player and for those watching or listening. I have shared many techniques in my other books, but in this book I'd like to focus on three techniques to include in your playing: the 'Flamenco strum', the 'Triplet', and the 'Double Quick Flicker'. With each technique there is at least one exercise to practise and then a song to bring the technique into an ordinary playing situation.

Listen to the CD first. You may find that certain things will sink in without having to study the book in its own right. This will really speed up the learning process. See what you like the sound of on the CD, then follow the book, and keep referring back to the CD to check you're getting it right!

I've only just discovered some of the tips and tricks in this book myself very recently, and I've been playing for over 40 years! I hope some of the instructions and advice will reveal a new freshness to your playing and see you blossom as you discover your own playing style.

I'm thrilled that a great Tango beat instrumental called 'Boulevard' by Gavin Underhill, which featured on my album *Acer Glade* has been allowed into this book by way of kind permission along with 'Full Circle', a single I released recently. Broadcaster/TV Presenter Nicky Campbell has also allowed me to include his self-penned song 'One Last You And One Last Me' to demonstrate the 'Triplet' technique.

I hope this book will inspire you and unlock some great ideas within you. Remember: practice produces players!

Best wishes,

Steven Sproat

Overview of the Basics

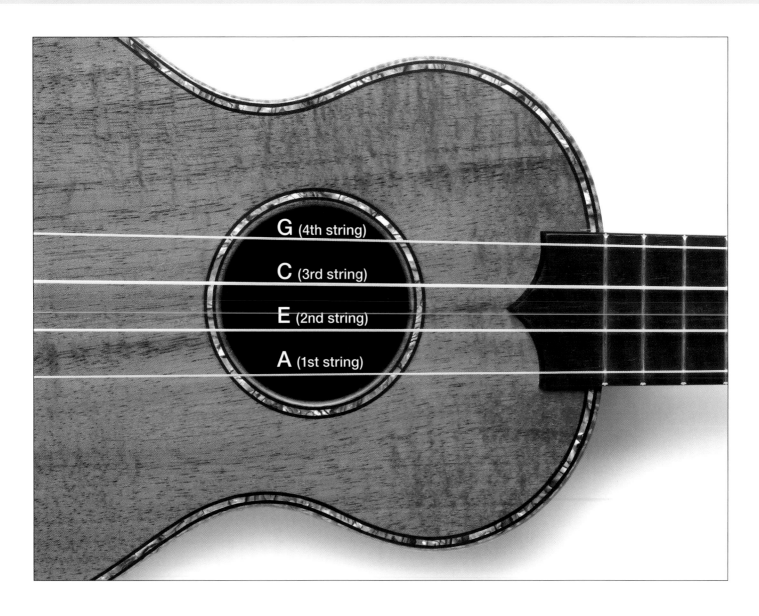

G (4th string)

C (3rd string)

E (2nd string)

A (1st string)

Tuning

This is by far the most popular way of tuning the ukulele. It's sometimes referred to as the 'C' tuning. Listen to the CD to hear how the notes should sound.

People often ask if ukulele chords are the same as guitar chords. I think what is meant by that is: if a uke player and a guitarist played the same piece of music, would it sound the same? The answer is yes, so long as the uke player is tuned to the C tuning and is playing the correct uke chords, as opposed to copying the guitarist and doing their own shortened version of guitar chords! Guitar chords are very similar in shape and appearance to a lot of ukulele chords, but the pitch and tuning of a guitar, being a bigger instrument, is different.

The chord shape or fingerings are often the same to look at, but a D chord on a guitar, for example, would need to be a D chord on the ukulele and that means a different shape. The chord of D on the guitar is the same shape as the chord of G on the ukulele, so it's important to learn the names of uke chords in their own right. It would also be worth getting hold of a ukulele chord book or chord dictionary (such as the *Gig Bag Book Of Ukulele Picture Chords*, Wise Publications, AM987360).

There are other tunings which are used (particularly by fans of George Formby) which are sometimes found in old ukulele sheet music and songbooks, but as the uke has gained in popularity worldwide it's now widely accepted that most players use the common tuning as pictured.

Tuners

Tuners come in various sizes and types these days. Most electronic tuners are the 'headstock' type which clip onto the peghead of a ukulele or guitar, making it easy to see the illuminated display and therefore easy to tune to the various notes. Some tuners are dedicated to ukulele, but most are suitable for several instruments such as ukulele, guitar and violin etc.

Consult your local music shop and ask to see the various types and how they work.

Strings

Many good-quality sets of ukulele strings are now available. It's worth experimenting with different brands and types. Everyone has a sound in mind that they would like to get near. A few good makes include Aquila, Worth, Martin and Keoloha.

If you bought a fairly inexpensive instrument to get you started, the chances are it won't be fitted with the best possible strings and so it's worth seeing if a good-quality set of strings might improve the volume and tone of your uke. It may even stay in tune more easily too, as usually good-quality strings are made from more reliable materials.

Holding the Ukulele

It might sound easy, but holding a uke in the correct way is important. Usually the uke is held as horizontal as possible just above the waistline. The right arm clutches the uke body between the forearm and bicep muscle, slightly pulling the uke towards the ribcage whilst the left hand acts as a balance with the thumb allowed to relax over the headstock.

We are all blessed in different ways and there may be some variations on the above depending on your body size and shape! Most importantly you should be comfortable and free to strum.

The Ukulele Family

Soprano

The soprano is the 'normal' ukulele size, the most traditional and by far the most popular.

Concert

The concert has a slightly bigger body and is longer in length.

Tenor

The tenor is becoming popular with guitarists as it has a much wider fretboard, and along with a bigger body, offers a wide variety of sounds and individual notes.

Baritone

You can also get a baritone ukulele, which is the largest of the ukulele family and about the size of a small guitar. Baritones can be tuned in several ways and have a much deeper sound than the soprano because of the size of the instrument.

Six-String Tenor

The six-string is like the tenor but with two additional strings complementing the C and A strings with a higher-sounding octave string. I have only discovered the six-string in the last year or so, but now play them all the time as they have a full sound that stands up on its own, with something of the quality of mandolin and guitar thrown in.

Banjo Ukulele/Ukulele Banjo

Often also known as the 'Banjulele', or uke banjo/ banjo uke, this is the uke that George Formby is most well-known for using. It is really a cross between a full-size banjo and a normal soprano ukulele, but it is much louder than a traditional uke. The older instruments (Gibson, Ludwig, Abbot and Dallas) are generally finer instruments than factory-produced banjo ukes, even though those factories might be making superb wooden ukuleles.

There are a few banjo/guitar/mandolin luthiers making fine banjo uke replicas including Phil Cartwright and Phil Davidson, who are both based in Gloucestershire, England.

Commonly Used Ukulele Chords

Ukulele chords are usually represented by a 'chord box' diagram. The vertical lines represent the four strings on the ukulele and the horizontal lines represent the frets on the fingerboard, beginning at the 'nut'.

Whoever invented this way of showing where to position your fingers to form chords decided to show the fretboard as if one were to play the instrument pointed vertically, but of course we tend to play the ukulele horizontally, so in your mind you have to flip the diagram on its side to understand which fingers to put over the strings. Here are some standard chords you should learn:

C

C7

D

D7

Dm

E

E7

Em

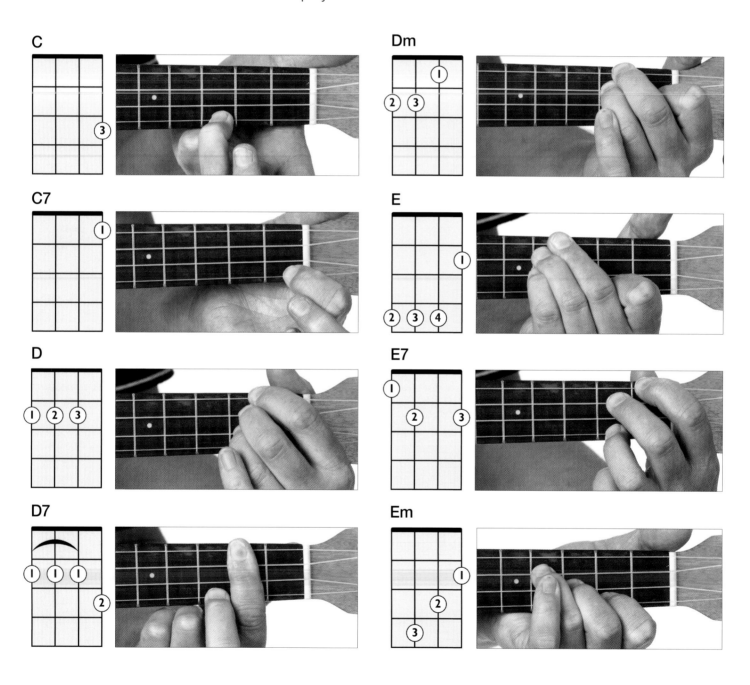

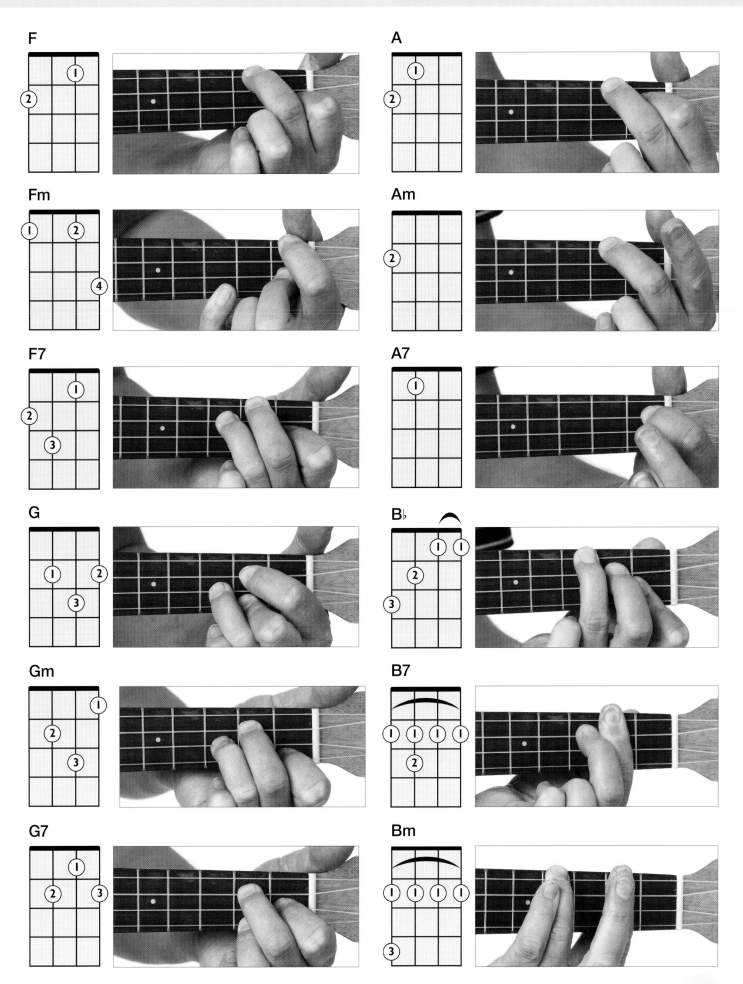

F

Fm

F7

G

Gm

G7

A

Am

A7

B♭

B7

Bm

Nails, Plectrums and Strumming

If, like me, your nails tend to split easily or break (or perhaps you bite them) then there is hope! Only very recently, I discovered the amazing advantage of having an acrylic gel fixed to the real nail of my index finger. It has boosted my playing confidence, along with increased volume and a percussive effect produced from the hardness of the acrylic upon the strings.

It's inexpensive, it only takes 15 minutes once a month or so and most towns have a good nail or beauty salon where this gel can be applied.

It's good to keep the nails of your left hand short as they can otherwise interfere with the strings you're holding down.

Other options

Felt plectrums offer a smooth, somewhat dampened jazz sound (Elias Sibley is a uke virtuoso who uses his own brand of green felt plectrums). They can vary in size and flexibility. Ideally a felt plectrum needs a bit of give and shouldn't be too rigid. Please refer to the 'web check' on page 38 for Elias's website.

Practising With Card

One of the early tips I was given in the 1970s was to practise learning strums on a piece of semi-rigid cardboard, maybe the thickness of a business card. At school I used to practise strokes on a bit of old card, keen as I was, to perfect some of Formby's techniques between lessons.

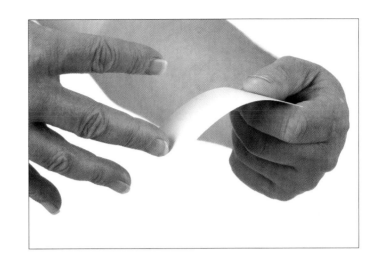

Watch Yourself

This might sound vain, but looking at yourself in a full-length mirror while you play can give you an idea of what the audience sees. You need to look comfortable and relaxed when you are playing.

Take Things Slowly

Whenever you are learning a piece of music or a song, take it slowly and perhaps tackle things a section at a time, especially any difficult chords or strums. Learn the music well. For example, get to know the songs and exercises in this book by listening to the CD several times before attempting to play; it will make learning much easier and more effective.

Strum Patterns

All music and songs have a given number of beats to the bar which is known as the 'time signature'. Bars contain a variety of notes—even different lengths of note—but ultimately the beat or count is often '1, 2, 3, 4' to the bar. The tempo of the song isn't important; the '1, 2, 3, 4' is counted accordingly.

For example, let's have a look at a basic down-strum pattern.

Using the nail of the index finger, strike the strings over the point where the fretboard meets the body of the ukulele (see photo). Never try and strum over the soundhole area; the strings are too high above the body here. It's easier, and produces a sweeter sound if you strum over the fingerboard area.

 4/4 Downbeat Strum

With four beats to the bar, this is the basic downbeat strum for a lot of songs.

Let's try this using the chord of F:

F

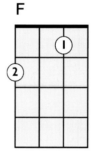

With this strum you can either let your thumb support and rest on your index finger like this:

Or you can keep your thumb away like this:

It doesn't really matter at this stage. Some players let their other fingers curl into the palm of their hand, and some prefer to let their other fingers point outwards away from the palm. Personally, I prefer the fingers clutched away into the palm, but uke playing is about being comfortable and being able to express a loose, chilled-out rhythm, so find out which is best for you.

Regular 4/4 Down/Up Strum

You can count the main downbeats as '1, 2, 3, 4' in your head and keep the up-strums uncounted; or you may prefer to count '1-and-2-and-3-and-4-and'; whichever you find easiest.

Let's use the chord of F again:

F

| ▼ | ▲ | ▼ | ▲ | ▼ | ▲ | ▼ | ▲ | ▼ | ▲ | ▼ | ▲ | ▼ | ▲ | ▼ | ▲ | ▼ | ▲ | ▼ | ▲ | ▼ | ▲ | ▼ | ▲ | ▼ | ▲ | ▼ | ▲ | ▼ | ▲ | ▼ | ▲ |
| 1 | + | 2 | + | 3 | + | 4 | + | 1 | + | 2 | + | 3 | + | 4 | + | 1 | + | 2 | + | 3 | + | 4 | + | 1 | + | 2 | + | 3 | + | 4 | + |

This should always come from the wrist, rather than the forearm. You need to feel the nice glide and watch yourself in a mirror as you strum. Remember, play down-strums with the nail and up-strums with the soft part of the finger.

You can practise strumming on the back of the uke. Turn it the wrong way round; there are no strings to get in the way. Once you feel you've loosened up, try playing again on the strings, sometimes playing hard, sometimes backing off and playing quieter, softer strums. Playing loud and soft (or quiet) adds feeling and colour to your playing.

'Skip' Strum

This simple strum is essentially the first pattern of four down-strokes with a strong upbeat strum after the fourth downbeat. Listen to track 4 on the CD for an example.

C

Let's try using the chord of C for this one:

C

| ▼ | ▼ | ▼ | ▼ | ▲ | ▼ | ▼ | ▼ | ▼ | ▲ | ▼ | ▼ | ▼ | ▼ | ▲ | ▼ | ▼ | ▼ | ▼ | ▲ |
| 1 | 2 | 3 | 4 | + | 1 | 2 | 3 | 4 | + | 1 | 2 | 3 | 4 | + | 1 | 2 | 3 | 4 | + |

This is worth learning as it will fit a lot of medium-slow tempo songs and is fairly straightforward. 'When I'm Sixty-Four' by The Beatles is a good example of where this strum could be used in a song.

Rock-Style Strum

Guitarists normally strum using a hard plastic plectrum and can achieve a loud, harsh sound because of this. For uke players not using a plectrum we have to use extra expression to compensate for the lack of volume. This is where the wonderful false nail comes into its own; it's like having a built-in plectrum on your finger!

This style of strumming uses an accented full down-strum followed by a softer down-strum, maybe only striking the 4th and 3rd strings.

Practise the pattern slowly. Eventually you won't have to think too much about it, as this is a stroke done more by feel than a perfect technique. Eventually build up your speed and put in plenty of attitude!

Have a listen to track 5 on the CD.

A good example of this driving rock beat would be 'Chasing Cars' by Snow Patrol or 'Yellow' by Coldplay.

A

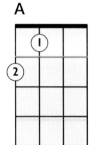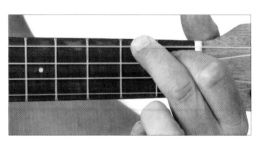

We're going to try using
the chord of A for this strum:

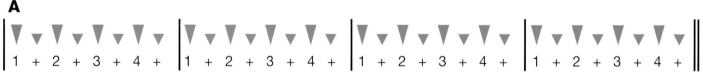

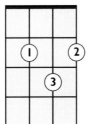 **Choppy Double Up-Strum**

This is an interesting strum that breaks up normal down/up-strumming. It creates an aural effect because of a split-second gap in the timing as one up-strum is followed by an up/down together to finish the pattern.

This needs to be practised slowly, maybe in two parts first. I've deliberately put a hyphen to represent the split-second pause. Again, do listen to the CD for an accurate example of this strum.

This sounds good on the chord of G so let's practise using this chord.

G

G

| ▼ | ▼ | ▲ | - | ▲ | ▼ | | ▼ | ▼ | ▲ | - | ▲ | ▼ | | ▼ | ▼ | ▲ | - | ▲ | ▼ | | ▼ | ▼ | ▲ | - | ▲ | ▼ |
| 1 | 2 | 3 | - | + | 4 | | 1 | 2 | 3 | - | + | 4 | | 1 | 2 | 3 | - | + | 4 | | 1 | 2 | 3 | - | + | 4 |

This strum pattern will fit classic songs such as 'Brown Eyed Girl' by Van Morrison and 'Sloop John B', a traditional song covered by The Beach Boys.

It's worth mentioning that as well as songs or patterns using 4/4 time—which is by far the most common—be aware that now and again you will come across songs that only have three beats to a bar, often known as 'Waltz' time. 'Delilah', 'Scarborough Fair' and 'My Bonnie Lies Over The Ocean', are all examples of songs that have only three beats to the bar.

You would tend to play a 'waltz' time song using straight down-strums of 3, i.e., 1, 2, 3, 1, 2, 3, 1, 2, 3 etc.

Flamenco Strum

I adapted this technique some years ago from learning the Formby 'fan' stroke. It evolved into what I thought sounded more contemporary and it adds both aural and visual interest, particularly for medium-slow tempo pieces.

Spanish-style guitarists have a technique which often incorporates splaying out the fingers one after another to create a roll sound. I've seen several styles and sometimes the thumb is involved too.

I eventually settled on the hard sound of the fingernails coming into contact with the strings, followed by the soft pad of the thumb to give a softer finish.

This technique will take several weeks to perfect, but give it time and keep coming back to it, who knows, you might invent your own stroke in the process!

The technique

The wrist is positioned high away from the uke with all the fingers and thumb stretched out:

Initially, just practise this part of the technique (the hardest part) and get used to your fingernails coming into contact with the strings followed by the soft pad of your thumb. It should produce a harsh sound, slightly aggressive, which is what it is really: a strum with a bit of attitude.

Once you feel you've got this part right, move on to learn the full technique.

The full technique requires some extra up and downbeats after the Flamenco part which finishes off the beat. Notice here how we have the curious situation of two up-strokes one after the other.

Do be aware that what follows the Flamenco strum can vary depending on the piece you're playing and also the timing. Sometimes the ending might be slightly longer or you might need to adjust to fit the music accordingly. What I have given you is a model to work from, so be flexible.

Don't overdo a technique so it becomes boring. Try and vary your playing, perhaps by bringing in the technique in moderation rather than using it in every bar. The exercise and song below are examples of where it fits, but I wouldn't normally play the stroke in every bar. I would tend to alternate between some general down/up-strumming and introduce Flamenco as an embellishment.

Here's a good example of how you might typically strum:
Start with a normal down-strum with the fingernail, then bring the wrist back into a high position to execute the Flamenco part—with the up-stroke closely following—then finally going back to do the final up and down-stroke.

Try this one on the chord of Cm, which has a natural Tango/Spanish sound:

Cm

Cm

To test out this strum, here's our first exercise:

It starts on a wonderful new chord I've discovered recently with a lovely haunting open sound. It's basically a twist on a normal C7 chord with one extra finger.

C7sus4

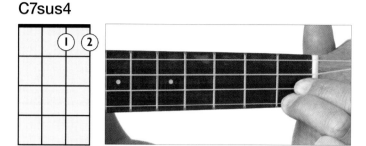

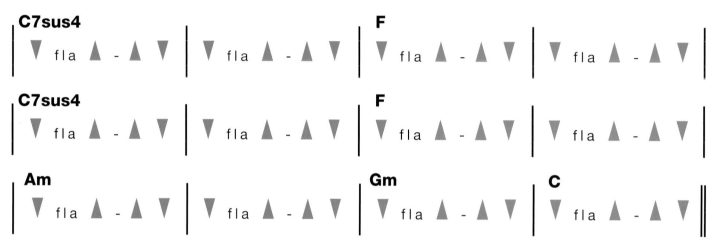

Learning a technique is one thing; being able to know when and where to use it in the context of a song is another. I recorded this song a few years ago on an album called *Acer Glade*. It was composed by Gavin Underhill, and Gavin kindly allowed me to do my own version featuring guitar and ukulele. I think it's a great piece of music, so give it a few listens to get used to it and then give it a try.

Boulevard

Music by Gavin Underhill
Arranged for ukulele and guitar by Steven Sproat

Main Body Riff
Start playing along after the 8 bar trumpet intro.

This sequence is played three times and then moves onto the bridge. However, when the song goes back to the start again for the second time it's only played through twice before going on to the bridge section the second time. The bridge also varies the second time and is played five times.

Part 1

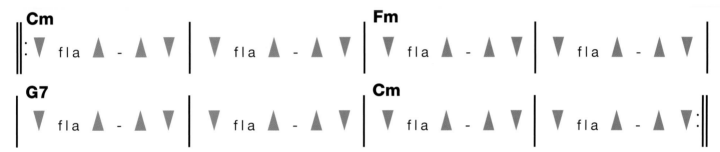

Play part 1 x 3 and then go to the Bridge.
Play x 2 the second time.

Bridge

Play the bridge x 3 before part 2 on the first time.
Play x 5 on the second time.

Part 2

Go back to the start to repeat.

End

23

Secret Chords

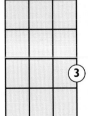

'Why secret?' you may ask!

Well, it's taken me many years to not only learn a lot of chords, but various different ways of playing them to add colour and expression. For example, I know about four ways of playing a C chord. It's the same chord, but can be played in various positions up the fretboard. I use these chords to add drama to a piece of music.

'Normal' C

Alternative high C

Often ukulele chord books can show many ways of playing common chords, but sometimes I've discovered by chance and by practice that my chords are not listed in uke books and therefore I call them 'secret chords'.

Here's a high sounding C chord, right up in the uke fretboard. Try playing it like this using your first finger on the 1st string, 7th fret and second finger on the 2nd string, 8th fret (CD track 11.) Now try changing between the normal C and then switching to the high C. Eventually you will commit it to memory and it will be there waiting to be exercised next time you play a piece of music with the chord of C in it!

Here's another:

'Normal' C7

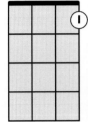

Alternative high C7

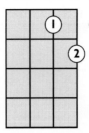

Place your first finger on the 2nd string, 6th fret then add your second finger on the 1st string at the 7th fret. It gives a lovely lift when you use this higher-sounding chord and it's good to alternate between the normal C7 and this one.

Here's one for when you come across the chord of A7:

'Normal' A7

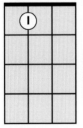

This is quite a common chord and this not only has a high quality about it but also a haunting openness. It sounds especially good on a six-string uke!

Alternative high A7

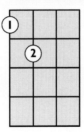

This version starts with first finger on the 4th string at the 6th fret and the second finger on the 3rd string, 7th fret.

If you've enjoyed the sound of some of these chords and wish to take your chord knowledge further please see *Absolute Beginners Ukulele Book 2*, (Wise Publications, AM996072) for more alternative chords (known as 'inversions').

Double Quick Flicker

This technique is an alternative to the Flamenco stroke and is useful as a stroke in its own right. It takes up the same number of beats as the Flamenco (and sounds very similar) but only involves one finger and some quick-time strums concentrated on the 1st and 2nd strings.

It's a very quick flick of a stroke and the pattern is shown below.

Try this on the chord of Cm:

Cm

Cm

I've deliberately used small arrows to visually get across the small beats this pattern has. For these double-quick down/up-strums we are only aiming to strike the first two strings or so. It happens so fast that these beats have to be almost flicked rather than strummed.

This will fit with a Tango beat like 'Boulevard'.

Again, like most techniques, there is some poetic licence, and you may have to slightly adapt the above model to suit a particular song. For example, it may end in an up/down after the double quick flick. Try it in different pieces and at different tempos, as it can be played either fast or slow.

The hard part is getting the timing right of the double quick flick. Think of the fast gallop of the 'William Tell Overture'.

Exercise

(13)

Bringing in the Flamenco or Double Quick Flicker

For either of these strokes be ready to do the technique almost straight after the first beat (I've shown this in bold type). Have a go at fitting one of these techniques into this sequence.

Siesta

Using Flamenco/Double Quick Flicker

C		E7	A7	F	G7	C	G7
1 2 3 4	**1** 2 3 4	**1** 2 3 4	**1** 2 3 4	**1** 2 3 4	**1** 2 3 4	**1** 2 3 4	**1** 2 3 4

Play the whole piece twice through.

Full Circle

First have a go at getting used to the chord changes and becoming familiar with the lyrics. Then, try either the Flamenco (which I used in this recording) or the Double Quick Flicker. Play the CD as loud as you can and strum along!

I deliberately haven't shown where all the Flamenco parts could potentially be played, as I'd like you to get a feel for when it should come in and have a go at placing it to produce an effective sound. It's very much down to feel rather than copying where to put it in line after line. Give the song at least three plays and by that time you will probably either recall my strums or hear where the breaks are. Have fun!

27

Full Circle

Full Circle

Words & Music by Steven Sproat

Intro Riff

Em		**B7**		**Em**		**B7**	
1 2 3 4	1 2 3 4	1 2 3 4	1 2 3 4	1 2 3 4	1 2 3 4	1 2 3 4	1 2 3 4

Verse 1

                  Em   **B7**
Who put the moon there? Who told the stars this is your space?

                  Em   **B7**
Who makes a sunrise? Who thought of night? Who thought of day?

  Am   **D**   **Em** **Am7 D**   **E**   **E7**
Oh, I'm just living like the rest,   lately thinking I'm not blessed.

Chorus

             Am   **D7**   **Bm**   **Em**
Do I have to go to school a-gain, maybe learn some golden rules a-gain,

             Am   **D**   **Em**   **E7**
Admit to being a fool, but then come full circle?

               Am D7   **Bm**   **Em**
Do I need to find an ali - bi, get a reason I can hide be-hind,

           Am   **D**   **Em**
If I find there's more to life and come full circle?

Riff

Em		**B7**		**Em**		**B7**	
1 2 3 4	1 2 3 4	1 2 3 4	1 2 3 4	1 2 3 4	1 2 3 4	1 2 3 4	1 2 3 4

Verse 2

             Em   **B7**
Who made these creatures? Giant whales that swim in the sea.

             Em   **B7**
These tiny insects, butter-flies, beetles and bees.

  Am   **D**   **Em Am** **D**   **E**   **E7**
Oh, I'm just living like you do,   lately searching for some truth.

Chorus

                           Am   **D**   **Bm**   **Em**
Do I have to go to school a-gain, maybe learn some golden rules a-gain,

                        Am   **D**   **Em**   **E7**
Admit to being a fool, but then I come full circle?

                            Am D   **Bm**   **Em**
Do I need to find an ali - bi, get a reason I can hide be-hind,

                      Am   **D**   **Em**
If I find there's more to life and come full circle?

Middle 8

   Am   **D**   **Bm**   **Em**   **Am**   **D**   **Bm**   **Em**
La la la la

             Am7   **D7**   **Bm7** **Em**   **Am7**
I'm going to keep up the search until I find my way

                 D   **Bm**   **Em**
Be still and listen to my heart

Am7   **D7**   **Bm7**   **Em**   **Am7**
In the silence of night maybe a still small voice

                 D   **E**   **E7**
Will call me to make a brand new start

Chorus

                           Am   **D**   **Bm**   **Em**
And if I have to go to school a-gain to learn some golden rules a-gain,

                        Am   **D**   **Em**   **E7**
Admit to being a fool, but then I come full circle?

                            Am D   **Bm**   **Em**
There'd be no need for ali - bis, no reason I should hide be-hind,

                      Am   **D**   **Em**
The higher life and higher climb complete the circle?

Outro

   Am   **D**   **Bm**   **Em**   **Am**   **D**   **Bm**   **Em**
La la la la *(to Fade)*

Fingerpicking

In my other books I looked at a six-beat fingerpicking pattern. The pattern below is only four beats and is quite easy to pick up.

If you are a guitarist then you may already have your own way of picking the strings which is fine. I tend to use just the index finger (I) and thumb (T) when picking a uke rather than using separate fingers but that's just because I was taught that way. Pluck the strings in this order: 1, 4, 2, 3. Follow the diagram below:

Four-beat fingerpicking

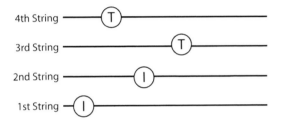

The sequence is 1st string, then 4th, 2nd and 3rd. Keep repeating this. Try it slowly before you build up speed. Eventually you'll do it without even thinking! It's actually easier the less you think about which strings you're picking and instead allow the feel and rhythm to take over.

Stand your middle two fingers below the soundhole (as shown in the photos) allowing your finger and thumb easy access to the strings ready for picking. If it's a 1st or 2nd string use your finger to pick in an upward motion. If it's a 3rd or 4th string use the pad or side of your thumb to pick in a downward motion.

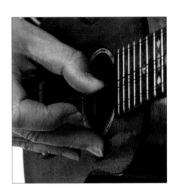

 Let's try on the chord of C:

Now let's try fingerpicking and chord changes at the same time. This might be a bit tricky at first but it will come together after a while. Keep practising and listening to the CD.

Here's our exercise called 'Siesta'. Remember: it's two bars of C, but the rest are only played for one bar each.

Fingerpicking Exercise – Siesta

```
‖: C          |           | E7        | A7        | F         | G7        | C         | G7        :‖
   1  4  2  3 | 1  4  2  3 | 1  4  2  3 | 1  4  2  3 | 1  4  2  3 | 1  4  2  3 | 1  4  2  3 | 1  4  2  3
```

Play the whole piece twice through.

Now let's try a song with this pattern.

This is a traditional song that has been covered by many artists including The Beach Boys and Johnny Cash (both versions vary in tempo). This version is intended to be a medium-slow speed and there are only three chords to this song, which is why I have chosen it, because we have to coordinate fingerpicking, chord changes and look at the lyrics.

Sloop John B
(Traditional)

Here is the fingerpicking pattern for this song. Each bar is doubled and is faster than the exercise we just played:

```
| 1  4  2  3  1  4  2  3 |
```

4 bars intro

Verse

G
We come on the Sloop John B, my grandfather and me

                  D7   **G**   **C**
Around Nassau town we did roam. Drinking all night. Got into a fight.

    G   **D7**   **G**
Well I feel so broke up, I wanna go home.

Chorus

So hoist up the John B sail, see how the main sail sets,

                    D7
Call for the captain ashore, let me go home.

    G   **C**
Let me go home, I wanna go home,

    G   **D7**   **G**
Well I feel so broke up, I wanna go home.

31

The Water Is Wide

I first heard this song on a James Taylor album called *New Moon Shine*. It's a traditional song, and his version is haunting and beautiful.

I've since heard the same tune put to the classic hymn 'When I Survey The Wondrous Cross'. You can choose which version you sing here.

Try this song two ways:

To strum, use the Choppy strum (DDU-UD); then try it fingerstyle, picking 1st, 4th, 2nd, 3rd etc.

The CD contains demonstrations of both techniques, followed by a backing track to have a go yourself.

I've included the wonderful C7sus4 chord which we looked at earlier, it just lifts the song. If you prefer you can use 'normal' C7. This song also has an open chord—Am7—which means no fingers!

There is a new chord here which is Cm7. It's a barre chord; in other words, one finger is used to cover all the strings. You may need to push your thumb at the back of the fretboard and press down hard with your finger to get a clean sound (see diagram). Sometimes to help press down I put my second finger over my first to act like a vice.

Cm7

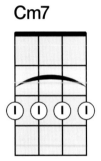

The Water Is Wide

(Traditional)

Intro Chords: note the lyrics come in on beats 3 and 4 to start the song.

4 bars intro

F	Csus4	F	Csus4	
1 4 2 3 1 4 2 3	1 4 2 3 1 4 2 3	1 4 2 3 1 4 2 3	1 4 2 3 1 4 2 3	etc.

The water...

    F   **C7sus4**   **F**   **Dm B♭**   **C**
The water is wide,   I can't cross over, and neither have   I wings to fly.

    Am7 Cm7   **Dm Gm7**   **Am7 C7sus4**   **F Csus4**
Bring me a boat   that can carry two,   and both shall row   my love and I.

    F   **C7sus4**   **F**   **Dm B♭**   **C**
There is a ship   and she sails the sea. She's loaded deep,   as deep can be.

    Am7 Cm7   **Dm Gm7**   **Am7 C7sus4**   **F**   **Csus4**
But not so deep   as the love I'm in.   I know not how   I sink or swim.

    F   **C7sus4**   **F**   **Dm B♭**   **C**
Oh love is handsome   and love is fine. The sweetest flower   when first is new.

    Am7 Cm7   **Dm Gm7**   **Am7 C7sus4**   **F**
But love grows old   and waxes cold   and fades a-way   like summer dew.

Alternative Lyrics:

When I survey the wondrous cross,
on which the Prince of glory died.
My richest gain I count but loss,
and poor contempt on all my pride.

See from his head, his hands, his feet,
sorrow and love flow mingling down.
Did e'er such love and sorrow meet,
or thorns compose so rich a crown?

Where the whole realm of nature mine,
that were an off'ring far too small.
Love so amazing, so divine,
demands my life, my soul, my all.

The Triplet (or 'slow thumb roll')

Out of all the ukulele strokes, this one, I think, is one of the prettiest and most satisfying to play. It relies on the late addition of the thumb following the forefinger to create a roll or ripple and is then followed by an up/down-strum.

It's a great technique to fill gaps or where there are no lyrics that can be added. It suits slow and medium tempo songs but does not work at a fast tempo.

The Technique

Start with the wrist positioned high up from the uke, as in the photo.

Notice how far apart the finger and thumb are at this starting position. It needs to begin like this. The finger strikes the strings as a normal down-strum followed by the pad of the thumb over the strings (mainly concentrated on the top two or three strings), then a quick up and down-stroke to finish.

To get you started there are usually a few beats
before the actual technique. This can usually be
two downbeats and an upbeat.
Here's the full example. The 'th' symbol means to
use the thumb here. Try it on the chord of F:

 ## Triplet Strum

Can you hear that the ripple or roll is coming in
on beats 3 and 4 so the first two beats are
fairly straight?

So it's '1, 2 and deedle de dum'.

Keep practising it; remember to keep your finger
and thumb spread out when you start the roll.

Here's a short riff exercise to try it out.
It's 4 beats for each chord; i.e., each bar has the
opportunity to play the triplet on the 3rd/4th beat.

Triplet Exercise

Play x 2

New Chords

C+

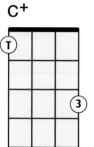 

Cmaj7

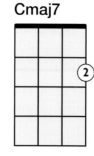 

D♭dim7

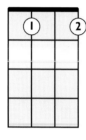 

E♭7

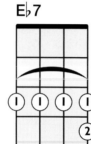 

 24-25 ## One Last You And One Last Me
Words & Music by Nicky Campbell

You won't have heard this song before, so listen to it a couple of times before trying to play so you can hear how it goes. It has a slightly jazzy feel about it, and some lovely chord changes, ideal for the Triplet technique to come through.

Intro

C				**C+**				**Cmaj7**				**C+**			
1	2	3	4	1	2	3	4	1	2	3	4	1	2	3	4

Verse 1

C   **C+**   **Cmaj7**   **A**
One last chance,   one last chance.

Dm   **B7**   **Em**   **A**
One last hope you'll change your mind, one last time.

Dm   **D♭dim7** **Dm** **F** **G7**
Baby, it's all   I'm ask-ing.

C   **C+** **Cmaj7**   **A**
One last kiss,   one last dance.

Dm   **E7**   **Am**   **E♭7**   **A**
One foolish notion that you're mine, one more time.

Dm   **G7**   **C** **G7**
One last chance to say good-bye.

Chorus

Gm7   **C7**   **F**   **D7**
All   those tears   in arrears, they'll cascade like rain.

Gm   **Am**   **D7**   **Gm** **D♭dim7**
If that is all,   let 'em fall,   no need for my re-frain.

Bridge

C **C+** **Cmaj7** **A** **Dm** **G7** **Dm** **G7**
Oh give me

Verse 2

C   **C+** **Cmaj7**   **A**
One last shot,   hell why not.

Dm   **B7**   **Em**   **A**
One last taste of what it was, all be-cause,

Dm   **D♭dim7** **Dm** **F**   **G7**
Darling we   were some-thing.

C   **C+** **Cmaj7**   **A**
One last go,   one last throw.

Dm   **E7**   **Am**   **E♭7**   **A**
One last no to all my pleas, she's got me down on my knees.

Dm   **G7**   **C**   **A**
One last you and one last me...

Well, you've made it this far! I really hope the book has unlocked some good ideas and inspired you. Do keep in touch; if you have any questions or want to know about gigs/CDs etc. you can contact me at sproatie@btinternet.com or through my website: www.stevensproat.com

Here are some useful websites:

UK Ukulele Festival
www.ukulelefestival.co.uk

Andy Eastwood
www.andyeastwood.com
Great player and great ukes for sale!

Gavin Underhill
www.gavinunderhill.co.uk

Elias Sibley
www.sibley-music.co.uk
Uke plectrums and information on Elias

Gabrielle Sproat
www.gabriellesproat.com
My daughter, who featured in *Starting Ukulele* and is someone to watch!

Nicky Campbell
www.mhormusic.com

Also By Steven Sproat

Absolute Beginners Ukulele
Book & CD
AM991804
9781847722768

Step-by-step pictures take you from first day exercises to playing along with a backing track.

Absolute Beginners has been designed to tell you everything you need to know from the very first time you pick up a ukulele.

Absolute Beginners Ukulele Book 2
Book & CD
AM996072
9781847728500

Step-by-step pages take you through the essential intermediate Ukulele techniques.

This book has been designed to tell you everything you need to know to add style and colour to your playing.

Absolute Beginners Ukulele – Manuscript Paper
AM1000010
9781849384711

This handy book contains 48 pages of manuscript paper, with two manuscript formats, specially prepared for Ukulele players.
Also including a tuning guide and chord reference library, this book contains everything you need to put your ideas onto paper.

Steven Sproat: Ukelounge DVD – The Complete Step-By-Step Guide To Playing The Ukulele
Catalogue No: 1094922282810

In this DVD, Uke master Steven Sproat covers everything you will need to learn the basics of Ukulele playing, right up to an advanced standard. It's the complete package!

CD Track Listing

The CD contains full demonstrations of all the pieces, plus backing tracks without the ukulele so you can play along. The demonstration will play first and then you will get to play along with the backing track.

Track

1	Tuning Notes
2	4/4 Downbeat Strum
3	Regular 4/4 Down/up Strum
4	'Skip' Strum
5	Rock-Style Strum
6	Choppy Double Up-Strum
7-8	Flamenco Strum
9-10	'Boulevard'
11	Secret Chords
12-13	Double Quick Flicker
14-15	'Full Circle'
16-17	Fingerpicking
18-19	'Sloop John B'
20-22	'The Water Is Wide'
23	Triplet Strum
24-25	'One Last You And One Last Me'

123456789